Decemb burning, our planes were exploding where they sat, and men were dying. I was so mad I didn't have time to be afraid."

That's how John Finn remembered the Japanese attack on the U.S. naval base at Pearl Harbor, Hawaii.

The U.S. Pacific Fleet

It was a beautiful Sunday morning. Almost the entire U.S. Pacific Fleet was at Pearl Harbor. There were about 130 ships and hundreds of planes, as well as about 18,000 military personnel.

The Enemy

Just 220 miles offshore, six Japanese aircraft carriers lay in wait. On their decks, 353 fighter planes from the Japanese Imperial Navy prepared to attack. By 6:20 A.M., planes were in the air, headed to Pearl Harbor.

The Attack

At 7:49 A.M., Japanese commander
Mitsuo Fuchida had Pearl Harbor in sight.
He radioed the order to attack: *"To! To! To!"*

The Americans were caught completely
by surprise.

4

The Question

What was it like that morning in
Pearl Harbor? Why would the slogan
"Remember Pearl Harbor" be repeated
so often for years to come?

PREVIEW PHOTOS

PAGE 1: A U.S. air base is attacked by Japanese bombers in this scene from the 2001 film *Pearl Harbor*.

PAGES 2-3: Japanese warplanes head toward Oahu in this scene from *Pearl Harbor*.

PAGES 4-5: Water sprays into the air as a torpedo hits the USS *West Virginia*. A Japanese fighter pilot took this photograph during the first minutes of the attack on Pearl Harbor.

Book Design: Red Herring Design/NYC **Photo Credits:** Photographs © 2012: Adam Chiu: 23; Alamy Images/Rick Pisio/RWP Photography: 37; Corbis Images: 21, 42 bottom left (Bettmann), 44 top (Museum of Flight), 41 (Smithsonian Institution); Everett Collection, Inc.: 10 (Buena Vista), 30, 43 bottom right; Getty Images: 12 bottom, 13 (AFP), 43 bottom left (American Stock), 1 (Andrew Cooper SMPSP/Touchstone Pictures and Jerry Bruckheimer, Inc.), 8, 43 top right (Hulton Archive), 40 (Edward Steichen/George Eastman House), 28 (US Navy/Time & Life Pictures); Kobal Collection/Picture Desk: 12 top (20th Century Fox), 2, 3, 16 (Andrew Cooper/Touchstone Pictures/Jerry Bruckheimer, Inc.), 20; National Archives and Records Administration: 34 background (Naval Historical Foundation), 44 bottom, 45 top; Naval Historical Center, Washington, DC/Naval Historical Foundation: 29; ShutterStock, Inc.: 42 top left (Kurt De Bruyn), back cover foreground (Inq), 42 center right (Valerie Potapova); Steve Firchow: back cover background, cover; Superstock, Inc.: 36; The Granger Collection, New York: 42 top right (ullstein bild), 24; U.S. Naval Historical Center/Naval History & Heritage Command: 33 (80-G-21743), 14 (80-G-71198), 4, 5, 42 center left, 43 top left, 45 bottom (Naval Historical Foundation), 38 (NH 62656), 26 (NH 92310); University of Hawaii at Manoa/Hawaii War Records Depository: 34 foreground (#126).

Maps by David Lindroth, Inc.

Library of Congress Cataloging-in-Publication Data
Dougherty, Steve, 1948-
Attack on Pearl Harbor : World War II strikes home in the USA / Steve Dougherty.
p. cm. — (Xbooks)
Includes bibliographical references and index.
ISBN-13 978-0-545-32930-9
ISBN-10 0-545-32930-2
1. Pearl Harbor (Hawaii), Attack on, 1941—Juvenile literature. 2.
World War, 1939-1945—Causes—Juvenile literature. 3. Japan—Foreign
relations—United States—Juvenile literature. 4. United
States—Foreign relations—Japan—Juvenile literature. I. Title.
D767.92.D665 2011
940.54'26693—dc22   2011003438

 Pages printed on 10% PCW recycled paper.

1 2 3 4 5 6 7 8 9 10   40   21 20 19 18 17 16 15 14 13 12

ATTACK ON PEARL HARBOR

World War II Strikes Home in the USA

STEVE DOUGHERTY

THESE WOMEN FIREFIGHTERS were among the hundreds of civilians, first responders, and members of the military who fought back when Pearl Harbor was attacked on December 7, 1941.

TABLE OF CONTENTS

JAPANESE FIGHTER PLANES roar over the island of Oahu in this scene from the 2001 movie *Pearl Harbor*.

1

"This Is No Drill!"

Pearl Harbor is under attack.

The U.S. fleet at Pearl Harbor was under attack! Japanese fighter planes shrieked overhead. Dive bombers swooped down over the harbor. They opened fire on U.S. airfields. Torpedo bombers attacked the fleet's seven massive battleships. It was chaos.

At first, some American civilians and sailors thought they were watching an air show. Then an announcement came over the loudspeakers: "Air raid, Pearl Harbor! This is no drill!"

Deafening explosions shook the harbor as ships

A U.S. AIRFIELD at Pearl Harbor is destroyed in this scene from the 1970 film *Tora! Tora! Tora!*

were hit. The sound of gunfire and screams filled the air. Nearly every American plane on the island was damaged or destroyed. U.S. battleships exploded in flames. Hundreds of sailors were killed instantly. Others died in fires or drowned.

"It was a pitiful, unholy mess," said one air-base commander.

HIDEKI TOJO was prime minister of Japan from 1941 to 1944.

World War II

What had led to this devastating attack?

In 1939, German dictator Adolf Hitler had invaded Poland. That invasion started World War II. Hitler's Nazi troops then rolled through Europe. Most of the continent was now under his thumb.

Meanwhile, in Japan, Prime Minister Hideki Tojo wanted to make his country the strongest force in Asia. In 1937, Japanese troops had invaded China, killing millions of people. They had then attacked other areas in the region. And Japan had joined Germany in an alliance called the Axis.

U.S. president Franklin D. Roosevelt backed the Allies. The Allies were a group of countries that opposed the Axis. But Roosevelt also pledged to stay out of the war. The U.S., he vowed, would "remain a neutral nation."

Still, Roosevelt had pushed back against Japan. He ordered the mighty U.S. Pacific Fleet to relocate closer to Japan. It moved from California to Pearl Harbor, on the island of Oahu, Hawaii.

Japan's leaders wanted the U.S. Navy out of their way. They planned a surprise attack on Pearl Harbor. That attack was now underway.

JAPANESE FIGHTER PLANES on an aircraft carrier in the Pacific Ocean prepare to take off for Pearl Harbor.

SOVIET
UNION

MANCHURIA

*Sakhalin
Island*

Kurile Islands

KOREA

JAPAN

Tokyo

C H I N A

Nanking

*Formosa
(Taiwan)*

P A C I F I C   O C E A N

Wake Island

FRENCH
INDOCHINA

PHILIPPINES

*Marianas
Islands*

Guam

*Caroline
Islands*

*Marshall
Islands*

BRITISH
MALAYA

*Gilbert
Islands*

D U T C H   E A S T   I N D I E S

Japanese Expansion Before Pearl Harbor

By late 1941, Japan's empire
stretched into China, Southeast
Asia, and the Pacific.

KEY

Japan as of 1894

Japanese Empire
as of December 6, 1941

⭐ national capital

0	800 mi.
0	800 km

A JAPANESE FIGHTER PLANE flies past burning U.S. ships in a scene from the film *Pearl Harbor*.

2

Chaos on Battleship Row

The USS *West Virginia* is blasted with bombs.

Mess attendant Doris "Dorie" Miller was in the laundry room of the USS *West Virginia* when an explosion knocked him off his feet. The tremendous blast sent shock waves through the ship.

Miller heard sailors shouting that the battleship was under attack. Enemy planes were bombing the fleet! Miller raced to a passageway, where he heard wounded men screaming and saw the dead bodies of shipmates.

The passageway was filling with thick black smoke. Miller inched along, searching for a way to the main deck.

When he got there, he couldn't believe his eyes.

Death and Destruction

The huge ship was leaning to one side. Its towering masts were broken. The ship's cannons had been destroyed. Everywhere, fires burned out of control.

Japanese fighter planes buzzed over Battleship Row. The USS *West Virginia* and six other battleships were moored there. Low-flying bombers torpedoed the *West Virginia*, blowing huge holes in its side.

U.S. sailors with their clothes on fire tried to put out the flames. Wounded men moaned in agony. There were dead bodies everywhere. The ship's deck was slick with blood.

Worse was yet to come. For the next two hours, the U.S. fleet was pounded by bombs and strafed by machine guns. But Dorie Miller and countless other servicepeople would not give up.

They fought back.

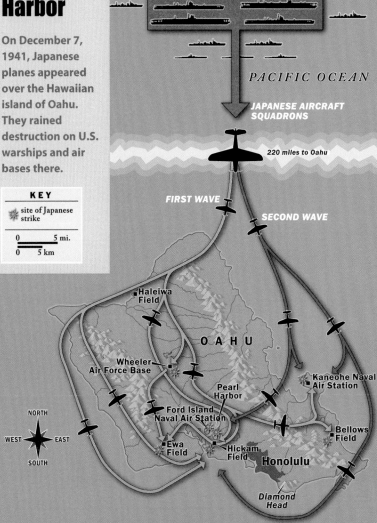

Attack on Pearl Harbor

On December 7, 1941, Japanese planes appeared over the Hawaiian island of Oahu. They rained destruction on U.S. warships and air bases there.

KEY

site of Japanese strike

0   5 mi.
0   5 km

JAPANESE ATTACK FLEET

JAPANESE AIRCRAFT CARRIERS

PACIFIC OCEAN

JAPANESE AIRCRAFT SQUADRONS

220 miles to Oahu

FIRST WAVE

SECOND WAVE

Haleiwa Field

O A H U

Wheeler Air Force Base

Kaneohe Naval Air Station

Pearl Harbor

Ford Island Naval Air Station

Bellows Field

Ewa Field

Hickam Field

Honolulu

NORTH
WEST — EAST
SOUTH

Diamond Head

THIS SHOT from the movie *Tora! Tora! Tora!* shows how Japanese fighter planes destroyed U.S. air bases. They wanted to prevent American pilots from taking off and fighting back.

3

U.S. Planes Attacked

**American pilots
race for their airplanes.**

Army pilots George S. Welch and Kenneth M.
Taylor had been out all night. On Saturday evening,
they had put on tuxedos and gone to a formal dance
at the Officer's Club at Wheeler Field. Then they'd
joined an all-night poker game.
Now it was early Sunday morning.
Welch and Taylor were debating

**PILOTS Kenneth Taylor (left)
and George Welch**

21

whether to go to bed or head out for a swim.

Suddenly, they heard an explosion. Wheeler Field was under attack!

Racing for the Air

Wheeler Field was one of five air bases dedicated to protecting the U.S. fleet at Pearl Harbor. But now Japanese planes were destroying U.S. planes where they sat. They were making it impossible for U.S. pilots to fight back.

Still, Taylor and Welch thought they had a shot at getting in the air. Their P-40 Warhawk fighter planes were at least ten miles away. They were parked at Haleiwa Field, an airstrip so small it didn't appear on most maps.

Taylor ran for his car, while Welch rushed to call Haleiwa. A crewman there told him that the airfield wasn't under attack—yet.

Taylor and Welch sped away, weaving around burning airplanes. When they reached Haleiwa, they rolled to a stop and ran to their planes. Still dressed in their tuxedos, the pilots prepared for takeoff.

The U.S. Fleet at Pearl Harbor

There were about 130 U.S. ships in the harbor
and hundreds of planes at nearby airfields.
Here's a look at some of them.

SHIPS

8	**battleships**	These large and powerful vessels had thick armor. Their giant cannons could pound the enemy from miles away.
8	**cruisers**	Cruisers were smaller than battleships. Some guarded aircraft carriers; others were used to attack enemy ships.
30	**destroyers**	Fast and compact, destroyers escorted larger warships and protected them from submarines and torpedo boats.
14	**minesweepers**	These small warships were used to find and destroy mines.
1	**hospital ship**	This floating hospital provided medical care for sick or injured sailors.

PLANES

113	**bombers**	Among them were 12 B-17D Flying Fortresses. They got their name because they were so well armored.
200	**fighter planes**	These included 23 F4F-3 Wildcats, the most common carrier-based fighter at the time.
105	**seaplanes**	Seaplanes can land on and take off from the water. Fifty-four of them were PBY-5 Catalina "flying boats."

AN ARMOR-PIERCING BOMB hit the ammunition hold of the USS *Arizona*. It set off a huge explosion that sank the ship in nine minutes. More than 1,150 crew members were killed.

4

Fire on the *Vestal*

**A brave captain
fights to save his ship.**

Cassin Young was the commander of the USS *Vestal*, a small repair ship. Young was belowdecks when two bombs struck. The *Vestal* was moored alongside the USS *Arizona* on Battleship Row.

Young immediately raced for the bridge—the raised command center of the ship. He grabbed an anti-aircraft gun and started shooting at the Japanese planes overhead.

"Good-bye"

A moment later, an armor-piercing bomb plunged through the upper decks of the *Arizona*. It exploded in the *Arizona*'s ammunition hold. The shock wave from the explosion blew Young and others on the *Vestal* overboard.

Within minutes, fires from the *Arizona* leaped over to the *Vestal*. The remaining crew prepared to abandon ship.

Young managed to swim back to his ship and climb aboard. He ordered his sailors to stay put.

Suddenly, a Japanese torpedo bomber turned toward the *Vestal*. Young and one of his officers watched as a torpedo dropped from the plane. It hit the water and streaked straight toward them. The two men glanced at each other. "Good-bye," Young said to the officer.

"Good-bye, Captain," the officer replied.

CASSIN YOUNG,
commander of the
USS *Vestal*

Battleship Row

The prime target of the Japanese attack was Battleship Row—seven massive warships lined up off Ford Island in the center of Pearl Harbor.

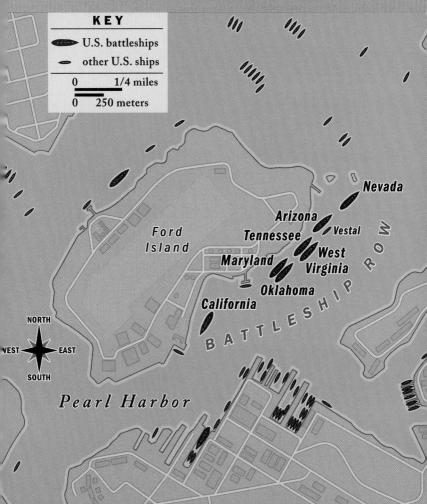

KEY

- U.S. battleships
- other U.S. ships

0	1/4 miles
0	250 meters

Ford Island

Nevada

Arizona

Vestal

Tennessee

West Virginia

Maryland

Oklahoma

California

BATTLESHIP ROW

NORTH

WEST · EAST

SOUTH

Pearl Harbor

A JAPANESE torpedo bomber flies through a hail of U.S. anti-aircraft fire during a 1944 naval battle in the Pacific.

A Near Miss

Young braced for the explosion as the torpedo streaked toward his ship. But as he and the officer watched in amazement, the torpedo shot beneath the *Vestal*. It struck the battleship *Arizona*. The powerful blast snuffed out most of the fires on the *Vestal*. But Young knew that to save his ship, he'd have to move it far from the burning *Arizona*.

Saving the Ship

The bomb-damaged *Vestal* was taking on more water every minute. Still, Young managed to move it across the harbor. Then, to keep it from sinking, he ran it aground.

"Despite severe enemy bombing . . . and his shocking experience of having been blown overboard," a military official wrote later, "Commander Young, with extreme coolness and calmness, [was able to] save his ship."

THE *VESTAL* after the attack. Commander Cassin Young saved the ship from sinking by running it aground.

IN THIS SCENE from the movie *Pearl Harbor*, Dorie Miller takes control of one of the *West Virginia's* machine guns.

5

In the Gunner's Seat

**Dorie Miller goes beyond
the call of duty.**

Two bombs and five torpedoes had slammed into
the *West Virginia*. Seawater was pouring in through
gaping holes in the side of the ship.

On the main deck, fires were raging. But Dorie
Miller ignored the danger. He rushed to move wounded
sailors to safer sections of the ship.

Then Miller heard a call for help. It came from
a sailor who was manning one of two big Browning
.50-caliber machine guns. The man operating the

second gun had been killed. Somebody had to take his place.

An officer standing nearby grabbed the second gun and ordered Miller to feed him ammunition.

A moment later, a bullet struck and killed the first gunner.

Miller froze. His instincts told him to take over. But he had no training with anti-aircraft guns or any other heavy weapons. As an African American sailor, he was permitted to assist gunners. But he wasn't allowed to fire the guns himself.

Racism in the Navy

In 1941, African Americans in the U.S. Navy were restricted to low-level jobs. They worked in the ship's laundry and kitchen or assisted officers. They weren't trained for combat. And they couldn't rise through the ranks to become officers. "If you were black," recalled one mess attendant, "you could only be a servant."

Still, Miller had watched closely at gunnery school as white sailors learned to fire Browning .50-caliber machine guns. And he was an excellent shot with a hunting rifle. As diving Japanese fighter planes called Zeros sprayed the deck with bullets, Miller climbed into the gunner's seat. He grabbed hold of the gun, took aim, and opened fire.

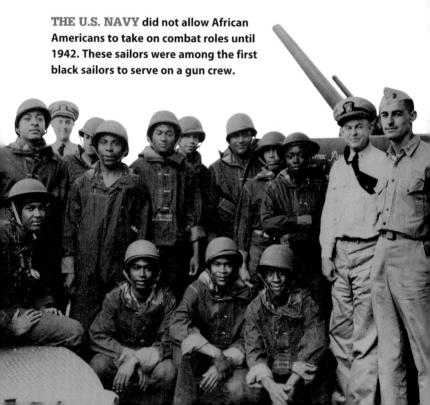

THE U.S. NAVY did not allow African Americans to take on combat roles until 1942. These sailors were among the first black sailors to serve on a gun crew.

PILOTS KENNETH TAYLOR (left foreground) and George Welch took to the sky to battle Japanese fighter planes.

6

Taking the Fight to the Air

Two U.S. pilots duel Japanese planes in the skies above Pearl Harbor.

Pilots George Welch and Kenneth Taylor took off in their P-40 Warhawk fighters. They climbed high over the island. Welch and Taylor searched the skies for enemy fighters. Soon, they spotted squadrons of Japanese planes far below.

The two Americans were vastly outnumbered. But they didn't hesitate. With machine guns blazing, the pilots dove straight at the enemy and shot down two dive bombers. Then they spotted another group of enemy planes and took off after them.

Dogfight

In a duel with a Japanese fighter plane, Taylor was wounded. His P-40 was badly shot up. Still, the 21-year-old pilot managed to shoot down the enemy plane.

At one point, Taylor took on a group of planes in a series of dizzying dogfights over the beach at Waialua. "I got [caught] in a string of six or eight planes," he recalled later. "I was on one plane's tail . . . and there was one following, firing at me."

THIS ZERO FIGHTER was one of 29 Japanese planes shot down on December 7.

Taylor tried to lose the plane behind him, but he couldn't get rid of it. He was sure he was doomed.

Then his friend Welch zoomed in and blasted the Japanese plane out of the sky.

The P-40 Warhawk

About half the U.S. planes at Pearl Harbor were P-40s. It was a no-frills fighter plane, but it got the job done.

Here's a look at why some pilots loved these fighters—and others hated them.

P-40 STATS
SEATS: 1
ENGINES: 1
(1,000 to 1,200 horsepower)
TOP SPEED: 340 mph
TOP ALTITUDE: 30,000 feet
WEIGHT: 8,058 pounds

STRENGTHS
SPEED: The P-40 could outrun the Japanese Zero, allowing U.S. pilots to escape dogfights when they were in trouble.

FIREPOWER: The aircraft was armed with two powerful .50-caliber machine guns and four .30-caliber machine guns.

AIR SUPPORT: The P-40 had thick armor and flew best at low altitudes, so it was often used to provide cover fire for troops on the ground.

COST: The plane was cheap to make. Almost 14,000 P-40s were built between 1939 and 1944.

GOOD TRACK RECORD: In early 1941, the Flying Tigers—a group of Americans piloting P-40s—volunteered to fight the Japanese in China. Although the Tigers were outnumbered, they shot down about 400 enemy aircraft while losing just 12 P-40s in combat.

WEAKNESSES
CLUMSY: The P-40 was heavy for a fighter plane, which meant it was clumsy at low speeds. It couldn't turn or climb nearly as quickly as the lightweight Zero.

SHORT RANGE: The P-40 couldn't fly very far without refueling. It was eventually replaced by the P-38, which the U.S. could use to strike targets deep inside enemy territory.

IN 1942, DORIE MILLER was awarded the Navy Cross for his outstanding bravery during the attack on Pearl Harbor. A year later, he was killed while serving on another ship in the Pacific.

7

Honoring the Brave

There were extraordinary acts of heroism on this tragic day.

Many sailors on the *West Virginia* prepared to abandon ship. But not Dorie Miller. He remained at his anti-aircraft gun, exposed to enemy bullets and the searing heat of fires burning around him.

A Japanese plane dove straight at him. It was coming in so low that Miller could see the pilot's face. The pilot fired his guns, and bullets slammed into the *West Virginia's* armor.

Defending the Fleet

Miller took aim. He held the big .50-caliber gun steady and fired.

The Japanese pilot unleashed a final volley of bullets at Miller. Then he pulled up and tried to soar away. But his plane had been hit. With smoke spewing from its tail, the aircraft spiraled into the harbor.

By some accounts, Miller shot down several planes that morning. "[He kept] blazing away, as though he had fired [an anti-aircraft gun] all his life," the officer next to Miller recalled.

Like Miller, hundreds of servicemen and women fought back bravely on December 7, 1941. In the face of tremendous danger, they did whatever they could to defend the fleet at Pearl Harbor. ✖

FILES

Timeline: World War II

1931: Japan invades the Chinese province of Manchuria.

1937: Japan conquers Nanjing, the capital of China, and massacres 200,000 Chinese civilians.

1939: World War II begins when Germany invades Poland. France and Britain declare war on Germany.

| 1931 | 1933 | 1937 | 1938 | 1939 | 1940 |

1938: The U.S. begins a massive build-up of its navy.

1940: Germany conquers France and other Western European nations.

1933: Adolf Hitler becomes chancellor of Germany. He turns the country into a police state with himself as its all-powerful leader.

1940: Japan joins the Axis powers (Germany and Italy) and occupies Indochina.

1942: The U.S. defeats Japan at the Battle of Midway, turning the war's momentum against Japan.

1944: The Allies land in Normandy, France, and begin to advance on Germany.

1945: U.S. planes firebomb Tokyo and other Japanese cities, causing great damage and killing hundreds of thousands of civilians.

1941: Germany invades the Soviet Union.

1942: The U.S. government orders the imprisonment of more than 110,000 Japanese Americans.

1945: Allied troops sweep into Germany. On April 30, Hitler commits suicide. Eight days later, Germany surrenders, ending the war in Europe.

1941   1942   1943   1944   1945

December 7, 1941: Japan attacks the U.S. fleet at Pearl Harbor. The next day, the U.S. declares war on Japan. It also joins the Allies in the war against Germany.

1943: The U.S. takes the island of Guadalcanal from the Japanese.

1945: On August 6 and 9, the U.S. drops atomic bombs on Hiroshima and Nagasaki, Japan. More than 220,000 Japanese are killed. On August 15, Japan surrenders, ending World War II.

The Enemy in the Air

Here's a look at the Japanese strike force that attacked Pearl Harbor.

MITSUBISHI A6M FIGHTER
Allied code name: "Zero" Zeros were more agile than any U.S. fighters at the time. The machine guns in their wings made them lethal.

NAKAJIMA B5N BOMBER
Allied code name: "Kate"
Some of these bombers were armed with torpedoes specially designed for Pearl Harbor's shallow waters. Others carried bombs that were dropped from high altitudes.

AICHI D3A DIVE BOMBER
Allied code name: "Val"

Val bombers streaked down out of the sky and came in low to hit their targets. The plane carried a big bomb under its fuselage and a smaller bomb under each wing. Vals were more accurate than high-altitude bombers, but they were also more vulnerable to anti-aircraft fire.

The Enemy at Sea

TYPE A KO-HYOTEKI MIDGET SUBMARINE

The Japanese navy attacked Pearl Harbor with five of these midget subs, which could hold two men and two torpedoes. Four of the subs were sunk or captured. The fifth might have fired its torpedoes into the USS *Oklahoma* and the USS *West Virginia*.

45

RESOURCES

Here's a selection of books and websites for more information about Pearl Harbor and World War II.

What to Read Next

NONFICTION

Adams, Simon. *World War II* (DK Eyewitness Books). New York: DK Publishing, 2004.

Allen, Thomas B. *Remember Pearl Harbor: Japanese and American Survivors Tell Their Stories.* Washington, DC: National Geographic Children's Books, 2001.

Ambrose, Stephen E. *The Good Fight: How World War II Was Won.* New York: Atheneum, 2001.

Dougherty, Steve. *Pearl Harbor: The U.S. Enters World War II.* New York: Franklin Watts, 2010.

Gorman, Jacqueline Laks. *Pearl Harbor: A Primary Source History* (In Their Own Words). Pleasantville, NY: Gareth Stevens Publishing, 2009.

Hoyt, Edwin P. *Pearl Harbor Attack.* New York: Sterling Point Books, 2008.

FICTION

Denenberg, Barry. *Early Sunday Morning: The Pearl Harbor Diary of Amber Billows, Hawaii 1941.* New York: Scholastic, 2001.

Mazer, Harry. *A Boy at War: A Novel of Pearl Harbor.* New York: Aladdin Paperbacks, 2002.

Websites

Expedition: Pearl Harbor
www.nationalgeo graphic.com/pearlharbor/ expedition.html
Follow a *National Geographic* explorer as he searches for the wreckage of ships sunk during the attack on Pearl Harbor.

The National World War II Museum
www.nationalww2 museum.org
This museum tells the stories of the 16 million Americans who fought in World War II with personal accounts, artifacts, photographs, and film footage.

USS *Arizona* Memorial
www.nps.gov/archive/usar/ home.htm
Find out about the National Park Service memorial built above the sunken USS *Arizona*.

aircraft carrier (AIR-kraft KA-ree-ur) *noun* a warship with a large, flat deck that aircraft take off from and land on

alliance (uh-LYE-uhnss) *noun* an agreement to join forces and work together

Allies (AL-eyes) *noun* the alliance of nations that fought against the Axis powers during World War II; the three major Allied powers were the United States, Great Britain, and the Soviet Union

altitude (AL-ti-tood) *noun* the height of something above the ground or water

ammunition hold (am-yuh-NISH-uhn HOLD) *noun* the place on a ship where ammunition is stored

anti-aircraft gun (AN-tee-AIR-kraft gun) *noun* a large gun designed to shoot down enemy aircraft

Axis (AK-siss) *noun* the alliance of nations opposed to the Allies during World War II; the three major Axis powers were Germany, Italy, and Japan

chaos (KAY-oss) *noun* total confusion

civilian (si-VIL-yuhn) *noun* a person who is not a member of the armed forces

devastating (DEV-uh-stay-ting) *adjective* highly destructive or damaging

dictator (DIK-tay-tur) *noun* a leader who has total authority over a country, often ruling through intimidation or force

dive bomber (DIVE BOM-ur) *noun* a plane that releases its bomb during a steep dive toward its target

dogfight (DAWG-fite) *noun* an aerial battle between fighter planes

fleet (FLEET) *noun* a group of ships, under one command

hangar (HANG-ur) *noun* a large building where aircraft are kept

mess attendant (MESS uh-TEN-dent) *noun* during World War II, a sailor who worked as a servant to officers on a ship; duties often included preparing meals, doing laundry, and cleaning living quarters

strafe (STRAYF) *verb* to attack with machine-gun fire from a low-flying aircraft

torpedo (tor-PEE-doh) *noun* an underwater missile that explodes when it hits a target

torpedo bomber (tor-PEE-doh BOM-ur) *noun* a bomber plane designed to attack ships by dropping torpedoes from the air

USS *abbreviation* United States Ship

INDEX

Metric Conversions

Feet to meters: 1 ft is about 0.3 m
Miles to kilometers: 1 mi is about 1.6 km
Pounds to kilograms: 1 lb is about 0.45 kg
Ounces to grams: 1 oz is about 28 g